Be My Moon

Also by Alexandra Vasiliu

Healing Words

Healing Is a Gift

Through the Heart's Eyes

Blooming

Plant Hope

Magnetic

Be My Moon

A Poetry Collection for Romantic Souls

Alexandra Vasiliu

Stairway Books
Boston

Be My Moon: *A Poetry Collection for Romantic Souls* by Alexandra
Vasiliu. Boston, Stairway Books, 2020

Editing services provided by Chris at
www.hiddengemsbooks.com
Cover illustration: ESZADesign via
www.shutterstock.com
Illustrations via www.shutterstock.com
ISBN-13: 9798553838713

*To all those
who hide the moon
in their hearts*

Contents

Be My Moon

*

My darling,
all I crave
is
to be your everlasting moon
and reign your nights
until the end of all darkness.

– *My Wish*

*

Last night,
you leaned over
and whispered in my ear,
"The moon never gets old,
my dear,
and neither does my love for you."

– *Words to Treasure*

*

Since my childhood,
I have been dreaming of
something wonderful
that waited for me
far beyond the horizon,
far beyond the sun and the moon,
something never before seen,
something amazing,
something that promised me,
"One day,
you will find the love
that you need."

– A Promise

*

Let me take you to the place
where all the worlds begin,

where the sky and the earth are portals
to something more beautiful.
Let me take you to love.
We will gaze at the moon
and the stars
for hours
and will feel
our hearts spreading light.
We will witness
that everything is made out of love,
and nothing is birthed
without hope.
Let me take you with me.

– Where All the Worlds Begin

*

There is no difference
between our hearts,
just as there is no space
between the moon and the night.

Our lungs breathe
the same dream.

Our mouths speak
the same language of love.

There is no difference
between our hopes.

We both wish
for relaxing Saturday mornings
when we can have breakfast in bed,
make silly plans,
and randomly laugh at nothing.

– *No Difference*

*

After your lips softly touched
my secret moon
like butterflies landing on roses,
I told you,
"I have never seen
anything more beautiful than this light
coming out of our hearts
and glowing in the darkness of night.
I have never seen
anything more passionate
than our smiles
protecting the miracle of our love."

– *A Magic Kiss*

*

When you seed kisses
in my heart,
your love eclipses
the seven wonders of the world.
You burn for me
and I can feel your heart
beating fiercely in every kiss.
Our love grows to new heights,
and I am not afraid,
even if we don't have wings to fly.
Is this how people feel
when they touch the edges
of the universe?

- *Passionately*

*

Whenever you tell me
that you love me,
I'm captured by your gaze
and in the blink of an eye,
I fall deep down inside you
like a shooting star.

I travel across an unknown sky
until I reach your heart.

"Open up
and let me in,"
I beg you.

Your heart is warm like a home.

I melt in your arms
like the moon fades
in sunlight.
I have everything at this moment.

Maybe this is heaven,
for I can't stop wondering,
"How can you make me dance
in such a beautiful way?"

– Love Is Like a Dance

*

All my life,
I have hidden the moon
in my chest
and carried her with me.

Although,
I kept one single hope alive—
one day,
somebody would be brave enough
to venture forth
in search of me.
One day,
somebody would see the moon
ensconced in my chest
and discover my magic.

One day,
somebody would choose
to spend
all the nights
of his life with me.

– I Hoped You Would See My Magic

*

Each night,
the moon tells me,
"You don't need perfection
to be beautiful.
All you need is
to keep your heart alive.
Let your innocence shine.
Everyone will admire
your self-confidence,
your mystery,
your magic,
your poetry.
Everyone will accept
that you don't need
unattainable standards

to be beautiful.
You can carry your flaws
and be partially hidden away
like a crescent moon
and still,
be wondrous like no other moon
in this universe.
Dear woman,
trust my words.
Stay simple,
kind,
and pure,
and you will always be beautiful."

– *To Be Beautiful*

*

Every night,
I pray
that you will hold me in your arms
like the night warmly holds the moon.
I thirst for your love.
I hunger for your joy.
I want to bloom for you.
I want to give you all of my heart.
Every night,
I pray
that you will hold me in your arms
like the night warmly holds the moon.

– Praying for Us

*

I love lying down
on the crescent moon
with you.

All worries are far away
from us there.

I chase love dreams
with you
until the light of dawn
enters our hearts.

I know
that in the morning,
we will be wrapped up in kisses.

My darling,
how could I ask
for anything else?
Life is at its best
when we spend our nights like that.

– *What I Love*

*

One night,
you told me,
"My darling,
all I want is to chase
beautiful dreams
with you.
I want to catch
tiny stars
for you
and display them
in your hair
like beautiful tropical flowers.
I want to follow their scent
and mystery
like a hungry wolf.

I want to swallow
every moonbeam
I find on your skin.
One by one,
until I become a burning flame.
I want to dress you up
with my light
and admire
your femininity.
My darling,
I promise,
I will love you
to the moon and back
every night and day.
And my love will make you
burn so brightly,
that there will never be
another moon like you."

– All I Want

*

The moon and the stars
are my witnesses to
how much I have searched for you.
Listen to their testimonies,
for they will not lie to you.

"She has stardust on her body,
moonlight in her heart,
flowers in her hair,
and wildfire in her desires.
She was so crazy
searching for you.
Every night
she was weeping and praying
to find you.

Hold her now.
She is trembling
and shivering.
Take her in your arms.
Warm her heart
with the light of your love.
There is no need
for the heat of the sun
since finding one another.

Look at her
with the eyes of love,
and everything else will deepen
in darkness,
fading into the background.
From now on,
she will be the queen
of your days and nights.
Let yourself get lost in her awe.
This life is given to you
to spread love
and be loved in return.
So let your heart blaze
through love."

– My Witnesses

*

I asked you,
"How can you love me
if you never see my other sides?
Maybe I am like the moon,
hiding shadows,
secrets,
or negative energies.
You only see what I want you to see."
You smiled at me and said,
"My darling, don't be childish.
Love is a mystery for me too.
Open your heart,
let go of these questions,
and let things flow.
If you wish to keep secrets,
then let me tell you

that they don't matter to me.
Even if your past is covered
in shadows,
you are plagued by ghosts,
or you harbor skeletons in your closet,
they can't tell me
anything meaningful about you.
I already know
that there is no other moon like you.
You reveal your femininity
in such an exquisite way
that it sweeps me off my feet.
I love you as you are,
full of contradictions,
naked, secretive, pure, and dark,
all at the same time.
You are my gem
and there is no other moon like you.
Never doubt my love."

– Love Is a Mystery

*

Once,
when moonbeams were shining
everywhere,
you told me,
"Come into my arms.
This night will be our cocoon,
our unique time
of happiness.
We are going to transform our hearts
into something different.
Tonight,
we will shape them
into butterflies.
We will fly toward cosmic flowers,
and live like

eternal creatures
made out of light.
We will dream of impossible things,
and our wishes will form
a new reality.
My love,
come into my arms.
Tonight shall be our cocoon,
our little seed of magic.

We will sow this sweet time
in our hearts
and create
something worth remembering.
Come with me
and let's dance
like butterflies
in the moonlight."

– Come into My Arms

*

I am not unattainable.
I am capable of giving love
and being loved.
I am merely a queen of dreams.
A moon.
A magic star
of light and strength.

My skin is a painting
that hides my femininity
within its canvas.

Come closer and see.

Under my skin,
I hide the moon.

Come closer.
I know that you long for me.
I know that you want
to see my purity.
My moon.
I can feel your awe.
Come closer.

My heart is spreading love,
whispering to you,
"I am the moon,
and I will attract you forever.
I am not unattainable.
I am capable of giving love
and being loved.
I am the moon
and I will always stay
magnetic,
beautiful,
mysterious,
magical,

electric,
bold,
pure,
energetic,
and powerful
for you.
Only for you.
I am the moon.
A special, unchanged moon.
I am your moon.
I will stay with you forever."

– Yours

*

When I go to bed,
I want you to stay with me.
Enter my dreams
and flitter around my fantasies.
Kiss my eyelids
and let your fingers play
in my hair.
Moonflowers will bloom in my heart.
Darling,
come closer
and stay with me.

The night is about to start.
There will be so much time
for love.

Stay with me
and carry me in your arms
to the moon and back.
It has been so long
since I saw
where the shooting stars live.

Stay with me.
I want to love you
with all my innocence.

Tonight,
we will look into
each other's souls
to find our magic.
And that will be our secret
to remember.

We will breathe as one
from beautiful united hearts.

– Stay with Me

*

This morning you told me,
"Your heart still has scars
from your past,
but darling,
even the moon doesn't carry
the shadows of yesterday.
Let me love you wildly
so my love can heal your wounds.
You know,
sometimes
I think that the stars are rifts
in the sky,
yet the sky bears them fearlessly
and beauty still comes out
of them.

That is what I want to do.
I want to infuse you with my love.
I want to make you shine,
no matter how many scars
you carry with you.
I want to make you believe
that you are magnificent,
no matter how many wounds
you still have to heal.

My darling,
let go of fears.

Let my love pass
through your wounds
and scars.
One day,
joy will come out
of your scars,
and your smile will be my reward."

– *Through Your Wounds*

*

If I were your moon,
I would always gravitate
toward you.

I would never fight
this attraction.
I would honor
all your wishes.

I would follow you
and happily tiptoe
behind you,
carrying my hopes
as though they were
the lightest luggage
in the world.

ALEXANDRA VASILIU

Day and night,
I would be there for you,
aching to offer you
all the poetry of my heart.

If I were your moon,
I would hug you
every night of the year,
all 365 of them.

I would stand without pretense
in front of you,
showing my raw purity
and my glowing beauty.

If I were your moon,
I would cuddle up with you
and share my impossible dreams.

I would laugh
while you counted
all the stars in my hair.

I would seek the sparkles
in your eyes

and the smiles
on your lips.

I would whisper your name
every night of the year,
all 365 of them.

I would unfailingly pull you into my magic
and indulge you with love.

If I were your moon,
wouldn't you be over the moon
with me?

– If I Were Your Moon

*

I don't want anything
in this world of avidity,
except for you.
I only want you.
I want to touch your soul.

Little do I know
of this impossible desire,
yet every night
the moonbeams show me
that miracles are still possible.

So here I am,
wanting to touch your soul
as I would kiss your skin.

I want to explore everything
that you keep hidden inside.
I want to dive into your feelings
and see
you still possess a clear path
to happiness.
I only want you.

I want to love
your cosmic soul,
your gem,
your purity,
your beauty,
your infinity housed
in your attractive body.

I want to hug you
with the arms of love
the same way the sky is destined
to embrace
the moon,
the stars,
and the whole universe.

I want to touch your soul
and whisper in your ear,
"You are a miracle.
And miracles are made
to be wanted forever."
I want to make you say,
"Your love is perfect."

In this world of avidity,
I only want you.

– I Only Want You

*

When I laid my head on your chest,
you patted my back
and told me,
"Darling,
you know,
you are like the moon.
You don't show me your whole heart
every day.
You are wild and magical
at the same time.
An unbelievable mix
of strength and beauty,
of chaos and harmony,
of music and poetry.
Darling,
I love you so much,

because you are like the moon
and don't show me your whole heart
every day.
But know,
though the moon hides her face at times,
she is very loved.
So stay as you are.
There is no other moon
more beautiful
than you.
Stay inscrutable as you are.
There is no other moon
more mysterious
than you.
Show me your grace,
even as you conceal your magic.
Whatever you do,
you will always be my moon.
And I will always desire you."

– You Are a Mystery to Me

*

At 2:00 a.m.,
I am looking out my window,
following the moon's path
in the sky.

I am so jealous of her life.

Since always,
the moon has been searching for
the night's arms.
Nothing more.
Nothing else.
A black-and-white world.
An everlasting quest
for simplicity.

How am I going to live
without this clarity?

I very much need
to live
in a black-and-white world.

No hues,
no colors,
no figurative meanings,
no multiple answers
to the same question.

Just a black-and-white life.

"I love you, honey."
"I love you too."
"I need to cuddle up with you."
"I need that too."

At 2:00 a.m.,
I crave simplicity.
Purity.
An innocent life with you.

I need you
just like the moon needs
to snuggle close to the pure night.

– Simplicity

*

If I were the moon,
I would like for you to be my sky.
No distance would divide us.
We would always be
of one breath
and one heart.
If I were the moon,
I would like for you to be my night.
No time would separate us.
We would fit perfectly
in each other's thoughts
and each other's dreams.
If I were the moon,
I would like for you to be my luminance.
No difference would disunite us.

We would forever mingle in light
and make moonbows together.
I would always shine on your heart,
full of joy,
and you would love me back,
making me feel
so precious and unique.
I would be your Silver Queen
and call you my prince.
We would be aware and admiring
of each other's magic.
And no sunset would keep us apart.
For in our love,
my darling,
there would be room
only for togetherness
and intimacy.
Neither you or I
would ever cast shade
upon our happiness.

- *Dreams*

*

Since my youth,
I have gazed longingly
at the moon's face.
"Dear Moon,
please
teach me
the ways of your femininity.
Teach me
the art of being beautiful
and mysterious
at the same time.
I wish to be like you.
I wish to possess
a magnetic beauty
which my lover cannot resist."

One day,
the Silver Queen
answered my pleas
and whispered,
"I will deliver to you
my magic,
my energy,
my power.
You will see all my romantic phases.
In each of them,
you will find my poetry.
I am the Queen of Longing and Love.
I am the Queen of Desires.

So here is my secret:
reflect your purity,
let your magic rise,
love your man,
be a love poem
in his arms.
There will be
no other moon like you.
Let me tell you,
my dear,
nights can be chilly
without me,
but they are spectacular
by virtue of love.
So stay busy loving your man.
Keep your emotions alive;
have faith
in love's healing power.
You will never be
an ordinary woman
again.
Love will transform you.
Love will make you beautiful
and mysterious
at the same time.

Love is the art of all arts.
So live for love, my dear."

Since then,
I have worked hard
to put the moon's words into practice.

When I fell in love
with you,
I slowly walked toward you
like a queen
bearing many lights and secrets.
I barely touched the ground;
nobody could hear my steps.

I felt so weightless.
"Where is the earth
when I look at you?"
I asked myself.
Your eyes were shining stars,
guiding me to you
through the maze of life.
"How can I breathe
when I look at you?"
I wondered.

Your passion burned down
everything around me.
We were the only living souls
in this universe.

I came closer.

I looked into your eyes,
standing fearless
in my full strength
and mystery.

There was no other moon like me.
I knew that.

And already I could see
your desire
shining over my heart.

I was ready
to be well loved by you.

I was ready
to offer you my entirety.

I was ready
to become your poem.

There was no other moon like me.
"I am here for you.
I am here to be your moon."

– *Let the Moon Teach You*

*

I will always remember
when you told me,
"I don't need
to steal the moon from the sky
to make you believe
in my love.
I will let you in
so you can see my heart
protecting the only beautiful moon
in this world.
You.
For that moon is you,
my darling.
Magnetic,
electrifying,

charming,
enticing,
elegant,
pure,
and beautiful
in all the ways
both possible and impossible.
You are my moon.
And I will never need
to steal the moon
from the sky,
for you are already
my magic,
my goddess,
my queen,
my love,
my everything.
And there is no magic,
no beauty,
and no other moon
like you.
My darling,
let my love be your sky.
Come here
in my arms

and let your soul shine.
Let no fear dim your magic.
I promise,
I will be your sky
for eternity
and make you believe
that in the whole universe
there is no other moon
like you."

I will always remember that night.

We matched perfectly.
Harmony was the name created for us.

— *We Create a Bliss Together*

*

Every night,
you try to woo me,
saying,
"You are so magical."

My dear,
I hold
thousands of dreams
behind my eyelids,
and myriad glowing desires
within my heart.

How could I be
anything other than magical?

Every night,
you whisper my name
in new ways,
until my heart glows
like a moonbow.

"You are so rare,"
you exclaim.

How could I be
anything other than rare?
A full moon has risen
inside my heart.

Every night,
you take your time
when you unbraid my hair.
The little stars hidden in my curls
always fall down
to the floor of our bedroom.

"I want to lose myself
in your beauty,"
you tell me.
How could you resist me?

You pour all the darkness of night
into glasses,
give a toast,
and then we drink it down
to the last sip.

"Let's melt together in love,"
you say.
"Joy will outshine everything."

Every night,
we are two crescent moons
entwined together in perfection.
And this is how
I become rare and magical
like no other moon in the world.

– *Every Night*

*

Let me be the queen
of your heart.
I will hold
the moon
within my soul
and hang
thousands of stars
around my heart.
I will exhale warmth
and devotion,
intricate beauty,
and irresistible music.
I will breathe in your hopes
and linger in your dreams.
I promise
I will be

the queen of your heart
and whisper your name
every night.

I promise
I will love you
so much and so deeply
that my love will be
the new North Star
for you.

All I need
is for you to give me
the sky—your whole heart.

Give me that,
and I will shine
like no other moon
in this world.

I will love you
in a way
that nobody else can love you.

And you will always bask in
my glowing beauty,
in my unique kind of love.
I promise
I will be
the queen of your heart.

– The Queen of Your Heart

*

Since I fell in love
with you,
I haven't had a fear of heights anymore.
I can touch the sky
with my heart
and hold the moon
in my hands.
I can fly
beyond the sun
and soak up all the light
in the pockets of my soul.
I can carry galaxies
in my hair
and still keep a cosmos flower
behind my ear.
I can come back to you

running on a rainbow
and bring you
never-before-seen moonflowers.

Since I fell in love
with you,
my heart
has grown wings.
I can do
all the extraordinary,
impossible,
heroic things
that have been written in books.
For this is the truth:
since I fell in love with you,
I became a miracle,
and so did you.

– Thank You for Your Love

*

In love,
don't look to the ground
if you want to see
how miracles come to life.

God gave you
the sky,
the sun,
the moon,
and the stars
to connect
with infinity.

They are part of your family.

In love,
look to the sky,
the sun,
the moon,
and the stars
for guidance.
Let them teach you
the art of keeping your hopes high.

In love,
you need to dream.

In love,
you will learn
how your heart can fly
without fears
or wings.

In love,
never look to the ground.
Love is made for the valiant hearts
that can carry
the stars and the moon
with them.
Be brave.
Dream.
Love.
And shine.

– Be Brave in Love

*

What I miss most about us
is the first night
we spent together,
when we gazed at stars
with misty eyes.
Suddenly,
in a magical way,
the night's darkness gave way to light
shining
all around us.

You smiled at me
and said,
"I only need
the moon,
two glasses of stars,

and our hearts on fire.
And I am going to change
the world
for the better,
for us."
I remember
how you took my hand,
held me in your arms tightly
and we started to dance
on a fragile moonbeam
suspended in the air.

You changed the sky into a dance floor
just for us.

"Where did the ceiling go?
Where are we?"
I asked myself.
I had no clue.

We were so young
and new to that cosmic marvel.

"Don't be afraid,"
you whispered in my ear.

"When I kiss you,
I will stop this moment forever."

Your eyes promised me
so many little moonstruck dreams.
I believed everything.
I wanted to save all your sweet words
deep down
in my heart.

You took my hand again
and helped me touch the summit
of every galaxy.
I couldn't be happier.

My lips grazed your eyelids.
"Dream of me,"
I said.

Your eyes noticed
millions of stars dressing me up
in beauty.

"You are wonderful,"
you murmured.

You kissed me
like an angel
and made our night last forever.

We were so young
and new to that cosmic marvel.
And this is what I truly miss about us.

– *The Cosmic Marvel*

*

I have always been
jealous of moonbeams,
for they could touch you
the way I wanted to touch you.

Eventually,
I learned to seed kisses
in your heart
in a clandestine way.

When the light between us grows,
I close my eyes
and hold your body
in my heart's embrace.
I draw you near me,
so near

that there is no space left
between us.

I am one with you.
I am one with love.
I am one with the moonbeams.
I am everywhere on your skin.
I am everywhere in your heart.
I can kiss you
like the light kisses you.

Eventually,
I turned my heart into your moon.

- *Jealous*

*

The nights are never too long
for your fingers
to reach my heart
and explore my depths,
in search of something precious.
"Where is your moon?"
you ask me.
"I want to find
the fountain of your innocence."

The nights are never too long
for my lips
to whisper to you,
"My heart is a mirror.
When you look at me,
you will only see my love

intertwined with yours.
When you search for my innocence,
you are hungry to find yours too.
When you want to find my moon,
you need to feel special too."

The nights are never too long
for our wishes to dance
in the rhythm of love.

– Never Too Long

*

You asked me,
"My darling,
tonight,
wear a nightgown
made of moonbeams.
I will seed
flower kisses
on your lips.
I will take
all the fragile parts of your soul
in my hands.
I will gently caress them
and make you shine again.
My darling,
tonight,
be beautiful for me;

be entirely mine.
I promise
I will make you bloom
like no other moon
in the sky."

And I whispered in your ear,
"Tonight,
I will be your goddess.
We will have all the time
in the world
to create
our kingdom of love."

– Tonight

*

Hold my hand, please.
I don't want to fall
from the planet
of never-ending dreams.

I want to be with you
for all the sunrises of your life.
We could chase love dreams
every day.

Hold me tight.

Hand in hand,
we will beat as one beautiful heart,
fulfilling our wishes.

Take my hand.

I want to show you the road
to our home
in the sky,
over clouds and stars,
behind the moon and sun.

On the planet of never-ending dreams,
we will dwell
like two children
waiting for happiness
to find its way to us.

– *Hand in Hand*

*

When the night warmly envelops
the moon
and the world cuddles up
with quietness,
I start thinking of you.
When everything is covered
with dreams,
I crave you so much.
My heart is like a hungry wolf
howling inconsolably,
asking,
"Where are you?
Are you also alone?
Do you miss my touch?
Do you remember my smiles?

Do you whisper my name
in the middle of the night?
Do you ever think of our dates?
What are you doing now?
Are you already in bed?
Are you dreaming of me?
Are you still waiting for me?"

When the night warmly envelops
the moon
and the world cuddles up
with quietness,
my heart starts searching for you.
When everything is covered
with dreams,
I yearn for you so much.
I hope
my longing will reach you
beyond distance and time.
And I hope you will come back to me.

– Like a Wolf

*

If you miss our rendezvous,
meet me
where the falling stars dance.
Wait for me there
day after day,
night after night.

Someday,
I will come
and show you
the magic stairway
to the *Land of Love*.

I believe
that we will find a way out
of this world

and fly
straight ahead to happiness.

In that moment,
we will link up in love
like colors becoming rainbows.

We will forever live
alongside the falling stars
in the *Land of Light*.

If you miss our rendezvous,
wait for me
where the falling stars dance.

– *If You Want to See Me*

*

My darling,
we always spend our nights
the way we would weave
beautiful dreams:
counting stars
on the sickle moon,
making childish wishes,
laughing at simple things,
and writing
I love you
on each other's back.

Our nights feel like
the only real thing
in this world.

Every morning,
we take these memories
with us,
trying not to lose our grip.

And during the day,
we keep kissing each other
within our hearts,
promising not to forget
or skip a night like this.

- *Always*

*

Do you still remember that night
in the forest
when we gazed at the stars
and the moon,
while countless fireflies
danced around us?

We shared
thousands of trifles,
kissed for hours,
and hoped
to be together
for the rest of our lives.
It has been one year since then,
or said another way,
365 moons ago.

Do you remember that night?

Do you want to go back in time?
We will be reliving
our crazy dreams of love
once again.

– 365 Moons Ago

*

Your love is so strong
that it can make the whole universe
a safe place for us.

You chose the sky
to be our best snuggling place.

It feels so good
to curl up with you,
so, so, so far away from Earth.

You chose a corner of the moon
to hold me in your arms.

I feel so blessed
to link your heart with mine

so, so, so far away from Earth.

With you,
life begins to be
so, so, so beautiful.

– *Your Love Is So Strong*

*

When the moon passes,
there are no more traces of it
in the sky.

"What remains after its leaving?"
you asked me.

"I don't know, my love.
Maybe just our wishes
tucked deep down
in our hearts."

"What is your biggest desire?"
you asked.

"I want you
to love me
with all your magical
and romantic hopes.
Love me beautifully.
This would be
the only way
you can leave a trace
of yourself
in my heart."

– The Only Trace

*

Be my ocean;
I will be your moon.

At dusk,
I will rise from your loving embrace,
uplifting you
with my beauty.

At dawn,
I will be submerged into your heart,
mingling my passion
with your emotions,
making you feel young again.

Be my ocean;
always look up at me

with love and warmth.

I will be your moon
and blanket your soul
with my grace
every single night.

– Your Moon

*

I will always remember the moment
when you promised me,

"For you,
I will hunt down the moon.
I will catch it
and offer it to you
as a diamond on your ring finger."

I will always remember the moment
when I believed you
with all my heart.

Some moments are so beautiful
that they don't seem real,
yet they are completely ours.

– *The Diamond Ring*

*

Inside my chest,
I hold the moon.

My heart is a secret sanctuary
where I dream of magic worlds.

Come closer,
enter my palace,
open the doors to my femininity,
and take a peek.
You might see
a canopy of twinkling stars
or even my little moon
calling you,
saying,

"Stay with me.
Don't leave.
We are meant to dream together."

– Holding the Moon

*

You have always told me,
"Darling,
you are so beautiful,
for your heart
is never devoid of love.
You emulate the sky
which at its lowest point
still carries
a full moon.
You are beautiful, my darling.
You are so beautiful."

– Your Words Shine

*

Every night,
I feel privileged
watching the moon
sinking beneath your skin.

Every morning,
I feel blessed
watching the sun
rising from your heart.

Every minute,
I feel happy
knowing both the sun and moon
guard all the secrets of our love.

– So Blessed

*

Just as the moon is looking for the night,
birds are looking for the sky.
And I am always looking for you,
only for you.

Just as the moon is one with the sky,
I crave the nearness of you,
the two of us together as one.
Nothing less.
Nothing more.

– One

*

You keep returning to me
as the moon faithfully returns
to the night's nest.
And I keep falling for you
each and every time.

– *In Love*

*

When the moon tells you poems,
close your eyes,
open your heart,
and listen to her enigmatic voice.
Don't be deaf to her magic words.
The moon will show you
that love has its own way
of knocking at your heart's door.
All you have to do
is to be home
in your heart.

Take a pen
and let the moon whisper her magic.

Write all the moon's words
upon your heart.
You must have a secret place
somewhere deep down
where you store
all your wishes.
Hide there these poems.
One day,
they will rise into your heart.

One day,
you will be thrilled
to share
all the moon's magic
with the world.
One day,
you will become a beautiful poem too.
A poem of love.
Everything else will be eclipsed.

– When the Moon Tells You Poems

Dear Reader,

Thank you very much for reading my book. If you are a moon lover just like me, I hope my poems resonated with you. If so, please take a moment and show your appreciation by writing a short Amazon review to reveal the magical poetry of your heart. Your enthusiasm and ongoing support mean everything to me.

May my moon poems shine on your heart always and carry you away to love and happiness.

Until then, stay beautiful and enchanting like the moon.

With love and poetry,
Alexandra

About the Author

An award-winning poet, writer, and wife, Alexandra Vasiliu is a firm believer in the healing power of love.

She double majored in literature and French for her undergraduate degree before pursuing her Ph.D. in Medieval Literature. She published the bestselling poetry books, *Healing Words*, *Be My Moon*, and *Healing Is a Gift*.

When she isn't busy writing, she loves collecting seashells and spending time with her family.

Stay connected with her through Instagram (@alexandravasiliuwriter) and Pinterest (@AlVasiliuWriter).

Visit her at alexandravasiliu.net.

Printed in Great Britain
by Amazon